MORE HORROR WRITING PROMPTS

77 Further Powerful Ideas To Inspire Your Fiction

by Rayne Hall

**MORE HORROR WRITING PROMPTS:
77 FURTHER POWERFUL IDEAS TO INSPIRE
YOUR FICTION**

by Rayne Hall and Mark Cassell

Book cover by Erica Syverson and Manuel Berbin

May 2018 Edition

ISBN-13: 978-1719282864

ISBN-10: 1719282862

British English.

INTRODUCTION

You can use this book as a follow-on to *Horror Writing Prompts,* or on its own. This time, I've teamed up with horror author Mark Cassell. We've pooled our creepiest, whackiest and scariest ideas to inspire your creativity.

This book is crammed with fertile seeds for fiction that will thrill, disturb or scare your readers. Each prompt comes with a wealth of suggestions for how you can develop it to suit the kind of story you want to write. Plant those seeds into the rich ground of your own imagination, and watch them grow.

All you need is a timer (such as a stopwatch, kitchen timer or computer app), and a keyboard or pen. Many writers find that their creativity flows best when they write by hand, but the choice is yours.

Step 1: Set the timer to 10 minutes. Pick a prompt at random, and jot down whatever ideas it suggests. Some prompts have pictures, and you choose whether to write about the complete image or to zoom in on any aspect of the picture that intrigues you. Without evaluating the ideas or censoring your thoughts, just keep the pen moving on the paper or the fingers dancing on the keyboard. This process is called 'freewriting'. Whenever your thoughts dry up, write "What if...?", a question that jumpstarts writers' imaginations. When the ten minutes are up, take a brief break.

Step 2: Read what you've written, and underline or highlight any phrases that excite you or pique your interest. Set the timer to 20 minutes. Now 'freewrite' about the underlined phrases. Let your imagination interpret them. Your thought journey may circle around the original prompt, or lead in new directions – either is fine. You can also ask yourself: How might this fit into a short story? How might this expand into a novel? How would this scenario play out in the fictional world I've created for my previous books? What would my series' characters think about this situation, and how would they respond? How could this be even worse? What excites me about this prompt? What experience does this remind me of? How does this relate to my job, my ambitions, my dilemmas, my childhood, my relationships, people I used to know? Which aspects arouse my emotions, and why? And of course, that Open-Sesame question: What if...?

I suggest 'freewriting' about several prompts – perhaps one every day – before you decide which idea to develop into a work of fiction. One of them may visit you in your dreams at night, or make your body tingle all over whenever you think of it. That's the one to choose. Start building a plot for it. Save the others so you can use them for future projects.

When reading the prompts, or when jotting down your spontaneous thoughts during Step 1, you may remember having read a story that deals with a similar topic, or wonder what happens if many writers use the same prompt. Don't worry about this. There are few completely new ideas in speculative fiction. I doubt any book exists that doesn't include some previously used components.

Indeed, many great works of horror fiction use the same basic premises to evoke primordial fears.

The key is to plant the idea seed into the fertile soil of your own imagination. What makes the story unique is the way you interpret the prompt, the context you place it in, and your individual author voice.

This method works well for getting creative juices flowing, for breaking through creative blocks, and for starting a new project.

Sometimes a suggestion will remind you of another prompt in this book, of an idea you had long ago, or perhaps even of a story you've already started to write. That's good. Ideas are like pieces of a jigsaw puzzle. When several of them click together, a picture starts to emerge, and the story takes shape fast.

The prompts in this collection work for all kinds of horror fiction – Psychological, Erotic, Splatterpunk and more – though not every prompt will suit every subgenre. If you interpret the prompts freely, you can also apply them to related genres like Dark Fantasy, Steampunk and Thrillers.

If you're in the middle of a novel, this collection is less suitable. You may find my book *Mid-Novel Writing Prompts* (Writer's Craft 23) more helpful.

Mark and I write in British English, with British spelling, grammar and punctuation. We've used the gender pronouns randomly, switching between 'she' and 'he'.

Now let's get started. Do you have the timer set and the pen at hand? Ready... go!

Rayne Hall

HORROR WRITING PROMPT #1

What happened here?

Art Jun-Pierre Shiozawa. Copyright Rayne Hall

Ideas you can use:

Where does this play out – in the character's home, or in a hotel room?

Does this transformation happen suddenly, or did it come about gradually, getting worse each morning as the character brushes his teeth?

Does the distorted reflection happen only in this particular mirror, or in all mirrors and reflective surfaces?

What if the real person undergoes the same transformation as his mirror image, but with a lapse of several hours or days? Perhaps the mirror foretells what will happen to him overnight.

If this particular mirror is the only surface reflecting the altered image, is this character the first to whom this has happened, or does it happen to everyone who looks into this mirror?

What causes the transformation? The house? The mirror? The act of brushing teeth? Something in the toothpaste?

Although the character in the picture is an adult man, feel free to write about a woman or a child if you prefer.

HORROR WRITING PROMPT #2

The character finds creepy-crawlies in his room. When he describes them and asks for advice, people make fun of him, because those critters are safe and not to be feared. Embarrassed, he puts up with them, and tries to show no fear, even though they multiply rapidly.

Only when his room is full of them does he find out that these particular creatures are not the harmless variety, but lethal.

Ideas you can use:

What kind of creepy-crawlies – bugs, centipedes, millipedes, spiders...? Choose a type of critter that you're familiar with, so you can describe its behaviour.

If you're brave, write about a type of creepy-crawly that creeps you out, because your own fear will give your writing deep veracity.

Where does the infestation happen – in the character's home, or in a place where he stays temporarily, such as a hotel room or a secret refuge?

Whom does he consult initially – neighbours, friends, a lover? Why does their mocking disdain affect him so?

Show how he tries to overcome his aversion to the creatures, how he fights to overcome his fear.

Show how they get worse and worse, either in number, in size or in behaviour... or possibly all three.

How does he find out that they really are dangerous? Does a local tell him? Does he find the information in a news article or on the internet? What if a friend from back home texts him, "I hope you're having a great time in such-and-such country, and take care to stay away from the deadly such-and-such bugs" – with a link to an illustrated news report about a rare lethal species that has been sighted in that country, with a serious warning not to stay in the same room as one. And the character is trapped in his room surrounded by dozens of those.

HORROR WRITING PROMPT #3

A character hides in this derelict building. Why, and from what? What's her experience in this abandoned, cold house?

Photo by Rayne Hall (copyright)

Ideas you can use:

How did she get there? Did she know about this house and deliberately come here to find shelter, or did she stumble across it by accident?

Is she alone, or is someone with her? A lover? An aged person? An animal? A child?

Is she a refuge from justice or an illegal immigrant? Perhaps a pair of lovers are fleeing from an incensed cuckolded husband, or a woman has abducted her daughter from the clutches of her abusive ex.

Describe the interior: the crumbling plaster, the fallen roof beams, the shattered tiles. Perhaps there are remnants of furniture and decaying textiles. She may find items that are simply bizarre, while others have a practical use.

For how long does she stay here?

How does she keep warm enough to survive? Does she dare to light a fire?

What does she do for food? Does she hunt or scavenge? If yes, does she have the skills? Will she risk being seen?

Why does the house have two entrance doors? Are the rooms connected internally?

What if someone – or something – else has also sought shelter in this building?

HORROR WRITING PROMPT #4

A character feels creeped out by neighbours who watch her every move. They take note of when she leaves the house and when she returns, who visits her and how long each guest stays, when the courier delivers a parcel and when and where she does her weekly shop. Whenever she deviates from her routine, the neighbours demand to know why.

She asks them to mind their own business, and they comply.

Then something bad happens in her home, and she wishes the neighbours were still watching, so they would realise something is wrong, and come to her rescue. But the neighbours now mind their own business.

Ideas you can use:

Why does the character live alone? Is this by choice, or the result of a traumatic event such as the death of loved ones or a divorce?

Who are the neighbours who are 'spying' on her? Why do they do this? Are they motivated by curiosity, compassion or moral righteousness? Perhaps there is just one neighbour, and she is bored or lonely? Or perhaps that single neighbour has developed a crush on her?

What is the bad thing that happens to her? Perhaps robbers or rapists have invaded her home, or perhaps a serial killer is keeping her prisoner in her own house, tormenting her for days before he will finally cut her throat? What if it's not just the character who's in danger, but her pet, her aged grandparent or her child?

What if the character desperately tries to signal to the neighbours somehow? What does she try? What if the neighbour sees the signal, but pointedly turns away?

HORROR WRITING PROMPT #5

Who is this widow, who is she waiting for, and why?

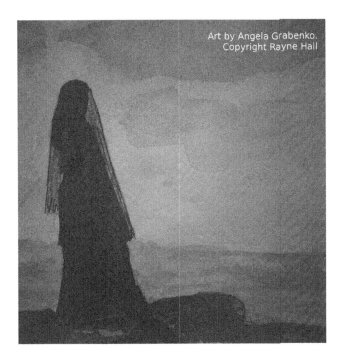

Art by Angela Grabenko.
Copyright Rayne Hall

Ideas you can use:

The widow could be the victim of someone (or something) who has observed her standing there every day and decided to take advantage.

However, she could also be a perpetrator, luring victims to captivity, death or some other horrible fate.

What if she's the decoy of a sinister organisation? Perhaps she belongs to a cult for which she lures new members (or victims).

Or what if she's a ghost? A vampire? An illusion?

Maybe she's a woman of flesh and blood who is trying to atone for an atrocious deed she has committed. What was that deed – the murder of her husband, perhaps? What must she do to atone? Why is this so difficult? Will she succeed?

HORROR WRITING PROMPT #6

You're a passenger. The driver acts strangely, and his behaviour gets increasingly alarming. You can control neither the driver nor the vehicle, and you can't get out.

Ideas you can use:

What kind of vehicle is it? A car, a motorbike, a horse-drawn cart, a train, a canoe, a plane? Where are you travelling?

What is the first sign of the driver's odd behaviour?

Build the clues to the driver's craziness gradually. Perhaps at first his behaviour strikes you simply as eccentric, then it makes you nervous, and finally it scares you into a state of terror.

You can increase the fear factor by letting the vehicle drive faster and faster.

Are there other passengers besides you? How do they respond? Do they share your alarm? Do they get worried before you do, or do they ignore the danger? What if the other passengers are weird, too? What if they and their behaviour remain so normal that it makes you wonder if you're crazy?

Do you manage to get out? If yes, does the vehicle continue to race to its doom?

Try writing this story in first person Point-of-View ('I'), but if this doesn't work for you, switch to third ('he/she').

You can end the story with the inevitability of doom, or you can end with the character's escape. If the character gets away, consider making the ending horrific because you have to leave something behind – a limb or a lover, perhaps.

15

HORROR WRITING PROMPT #7

What is this – a dental practice operating illegally without licence, or a torture chamber, or something different? What happens here?

Art by psionic.
Copyright Rayne Hall

Ideas you can use:

Many people have a great fear of dentists. You can tap into this fear and write a scary dentist story.

Why does a character opt for treatment by this dentist instead of going elsewhere? Is it a matter of cost? Does this dentist extract gold teeth for payment? What if the patient is an illegal immigrant himself, and can't risk consulting a licensed dentist?

What if the patient gets forced to come here, and struggles to break free?

What if it is not a dentist operating here, but some other business that makes use of a dentist chair?

Note the tiled floor, obviously intended for easy washing. Will a lot of blood need to get washed away? In most clinical settings, tiled floors are white, so any spot of dirt or blood is immediately visible and can get cleaned off. But here, the titles are dark and speckled – perhaps designed to hide bloodstains that haven't been fully washed away in the hurry?

What purpose do the hanging chains serve?

Who is the person in the doorway? Is it the dentist (or torturer), an assistant, a spy, a rescuer?

You can use the whole picture, or only a part of it, leaving out what doesn't fit into the story idea that emerges in your mind.

HORROR WRITING PROMPT #8

A character's attempts to be helpful are perceived as creepy. The more he tries to change that impression, the creepier he seems.

Ideas you can use:

What caused the misunderstanding in the first place?

What does he do that makes others think him a creep?

Who perceives him as creepy? The girl he tries to court, his neighbours, the whole community?

When and how does he find that others view him as creepy? How does that make him feel?

How does he try to change this impression? Think of several actions.

Why do those attempts get misconstrued? Is there a cultural misconception – based, perhaps, on different nationalities, different languages or different religions? Or does someone deliberately fuel the misconception?

HORROR WRITING PROMPT #9

Why is this girl bleeding? What happened?

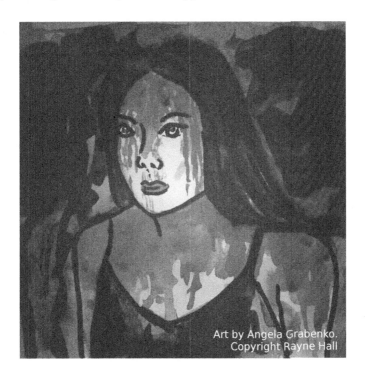

Art by Angela Grabenko. Copyright Rayne Hall

Ideas you can use:

Is it her own blood – or is it someone else's?

Scalp wounds often bleed profusely, even if the injury is superficial. Perhaps her head was hit or scratched. By what or by whom? Did she sustain any other injuries?

How does she feel – physically and emotionally?

HORROR WRITING PROMPT #10

A character travels and observes that one of their fellow passengers is distinctly creepy.

Ideas you can use:

What kind of vehicle is it? An airplane, a taxi, a bus, a stagecoach, a ferry?

In what way is that passenger creepy? Does he talk strangely, look odd, have an off-putting smell?

How does this creepiness escalate?

What is the reason for his creepiness? Is he sick, dead, a vampire, a zombie, a ghost, a paedophile, a serial killer?

Is that passenger aware of his own creepiness?

Are other passengers in the vehicle? Do they perceive the creepiness?

Describe the creepiness as the main character first observes it. Then let it escalate, so it gets worse and worse.

HORROR WRITING PROMPT #11

Who is this creature? What is it waiting for? What is it going to do?

Art by Jun-Pierre Shiozawa
Copyright Rayne Hall.

Ideas you can use:

How did this creature get into the house?

Is it waiting for anyone, or for a specific person?

What does it want? Revenge? Death? Blood?

Has the creature done the same to other humans? Are humans aware of the predator in the neighbourhood, and if yes, what precautions do they take? Do the precautions help at all, or are they useless?

Describe the moment when the people (or perhaps just the Point-of-View character) become aware of a presence. What alerts them? A sound? A smell?

How do they react?

HORROR WRITING PROMPT #12

A widower organises a trip/holiday/exploration as a memorial to his late wife. He invites all her friends/colleagues/supporters to join. A character who participate realises that the widower is a psychopath who is insanely jealous of anyone and anything his late wife had cared about, and intends to destroy them all.

Ideas you can use:

What kind of memorial event is it? A river cruise? A scientific expedition to the Antarctic? An archaeological dig? A rave party on a private island?

How does the widower select the participants? How does he persuade them to join?

Who is the main character of this story? If he's one of the participants, how and when does he get suspicious?

You can build the suspense by killing off the characters one by one. At first, it seems like a series of unfortunate accidents, then it appears the expedition is cursed. Then someone voices suspicions – and dies the next day.

Think of an unusual setting, perhaps one with strong atmosphere and inherent dangers: a raft on a crocodile-infested river, a mountain in the Himalayas, a log cabin far from any human settlement.

Why do the deaths not attract the attention of outsiders? Why don't the police investigate? Perhaps the remote location ensures that nobody knows what is happening.

This prompt has the potential to become a long story, perhaps a thriller novel. If you want to keep it short, you can scale it down by inviting only two guests to the memorial event.

HORROR WRITING PROMPT #13

Why are spiders crawling across this woman's face?

Art by Angela Grabenko.
Copyright Rayne Hall

Ideas you can use:

Perhaps the woman had a clear-out of her attic, cellar or garden shed. This destroyed the spiders' home, and they're panicking.

What if she hates spiders, and used a chemical spray or other method to eradicate them? Now they're furious and strike back.

What if the woman's enemy knows that her biggest fear is spiders, and deliberately puts her into a place and situation where spiders will crawl all over her?

HORROR WRITING PROMPT #14

During a long taxi journey, the passenger looks at the photo ID on the dashboard and realises that the driver is not the person in the photo.

Ideas you can use:

Who is the passenger? What is her destination?

How soon after entering the taxi does she notice the discrepancy? Perhaps she sees it the moment she's fastened her seatbelt, but the driver has already hit the accelerator/gas pedal. Or perhaps she pays no attention to the displayed ID until later in the journey when she gazes around out of boredom.

Why did the driver switch places?

What is his intent? Does he plan to rob, rape or murder his victim? Is he after a particular type of victim (e.g. young female foreigners) or anyone foolish enough to get into his car? Perhaps he wants to kidnap this particular passenger?

How did he persuade the real driver to give him his ID or his car? Perhaps he blackmailed or killed him. What if the real driver lies, drugged and trussed up, in the boot/trunk of the car? What if the real driver is an accomplice? Or perhaps the real driver is innocent but stupid, and let his mate have the taxi as a favour. It's also possible that the criminal pretends to be doing a favour to the real driver who may be intoxicated and unable to drive.

HORROR WRITING PROMPT #15

What was this now-derelict building once used for? What is happening inside now?

Photo by Rayne Hall (copyright)

Ideas you can use:

Was this an office block, a factory, a hospital, a sanatorium?

Why was it abandoned? Perhaps an economic crisis bankrupted businesses, or maybe an environmental or nuclear disaster left the town heavily polluted or radioactive.

What equipment and furniture might still be found inside?

Perhaps now it is a hideout for human traffickers, or a drug dealers' den. It could be the place where a paedophile, rapist or serial killer takes his victims.

Observe the windows. One still has curtains, another has a smashed glass plane, while a third is boarded up. Who boarded it up, and why – and why didn't they board up the rest of the windows?

The graffiti are in Cyrillic script – that's the alphabet used in Russia, Bulgaria, Ukraine, Macedonia, Mongolia and other countries in Eastern Europe and Asia. Perhaps the story takes place in one of those countries? Or perhaps the person who wrote the graffiti came from there?

The big, crossed-out word is 'Levski' – the name of a Bulgarian revolutionary who was hanged in 1873 at the age of 35. Could the secret activities in this building be politically motivated? What if the victims are political idealists, perhaps young people inspired by dreams of revolution and liberation, and the evil villain takes advantage of this and lures them to their doom?

HORROR WRITING PROMPT #16

A character turns up to someone's house for an appointment and discovers the door open.

Ideas you can use:

What is the appointment? Is it for a hairdresser, yoga, judo, driving lesson, or is it extra tuition for a child (the child could still be in the car)? Is the person owed money, or are they replying to an advert for the sale of a vehicle?

Inside, is there anyone home? Is there a stranger there? Does blood cover the furniture? Or perhaps their teacher/tutor/car seller is dead, or nearly dead. If it is a car or motorcycle sale, perhaps the character decides to take it for a drive. What could they find inside the glove box or in a pannier?

Does the character discover how their injured/slain tutor/mentor became an expert in their field? Now she faces a dilemma: does she call the police/ambulance, or does she steal the secret to become an expert herself?

HORROR WRITING PROMPT #17

Write about this demon.

Art by psionic.
Copyright Rayne Hall

Ideas you can use:

Does this demon always appear in this form – or does he have different looks, depending on who encounters him?

What does this demon want from humans?

Demons are crafty manipulators. How does this demon manipulate humans?

What would make a human comply with this demon's wishes? Perhaps the compliance is unwilling or unknowing.

What purpose do the horns on the demon's face serve?

Describe how the demon's voice sounds.

HORROR WRITING PROMPT #18

There is something in a glass cabinet and the character, likely a child, is tempted to find out what it is.

Ideas you can use:

Where is it? At home or at their grandparents' house, or at a babysitter's (neighbour)? Whatever it is falls on them, or spills, or breaks. Is it a family secret or heirloom, or ancient artefact?

Are they caught? How angry are the owners of the object, or were they not even aware of its existence? Perhaps they believe the child is not old enough (yet), or maybe unworthy to know of its secret or to use the item.

Later in life, maybe the object is once again found and brings back memories. What troubles could unfold for the person as an adult, what secrets could be unearthed?

HORROR WRITING PROMPT #19

What is this man going to do?

Art by Jun-Pierre Shiozawa.
Copyright Rayne Hall.

Ideas you can use:

Has this man been involved in an accident?

What if he caused it?

What if he came upon the accident and helped... or wreaked further damage?

Is he a mechanic who was called to the scene of the accident? If so, why is he topless instead of wearing a mechanic's typical overalls?

What if he's a road-rage driver who was so angry with other drivers that he hounded them until they had an accident – and then instead of aiding the injured, bludgeoned them with his tool?

Where is he headed now? To another car – one also involved in a crash, or one whose driver witnessed the event?

Think about the Point-of-View. From whose perspective might you tell this story?

HORROR WRITING PROMPT #20

When a character clears out her deceased parents' home, she discover a life-changing secret.

Ideas you can use:

Is the character alone, or is she sharing the clear-out task with a sibling?

Are the parents really dead, or are they in hiding due to this secret? Do their children later discover them to be alive after all? Perhaps their parents have gone on to the next plane (ghost story). Were the characters adopted, and when tracking down their birth parents learn how the people they thought were family were in fact nasty/outright evil? Perhaps the characters were actually kidnapped. Were their parents cannibals or murderers, or did they keep a creature or creatures in the attic?

If you discovered a family secret, what would you do? Depending on how it threatens the life you know, would you pursue it? Maybe you are in fact adopted yourself and so able to weave your experience into a horror story.

HORROR WRITING PROMPT #21

Why is this skeleton rising from the grave?

Art by Angela Grabenko.
Copyright Rayne Hall

Ideas you can use:

Is this a ghost, a zombie, or something else altogether?

What if it is the skeleton of someone who's been laid to rest – deliberately left half-buried? Why would someone do that?

If it's a ghost or zombie, what makes it rise? Is it rising for the first time ever – or does it rise whenever a certain trigger occurs?

Perhaps the rising is triggered by a phase of the moon or the playing of a certain instrument.

What if the haunting happens whenever a resident of that house is getting married – and the newlyweds never survive their wedding night?

HORROR WRITING PROMPT #22

A character's spouse obsesses over a new CCTV set up in their home.

Ideas you can use:

Is it rigged up in the garden or garage or nursey, or the basement/shed? Is this where he harbours a secret project? Is he holding someone captive? Perhaps he's creating something or growing a special/illegal crop? Is he growing or making drugs?

What would make him so defensive and obsessive? Has someone confronted him about it? Perhaps someone's contacted him, threatening to call the authorities.

Is the character caught intruding on their spouse's domain? Or does she quietly allow it to happen? How does this make the character feel? Betrayed, concerned, amused? Perhaps she's proud and helps her husband to further his project?

HORROR WRITING PROMPT #23

A character is held captive in this room.

Ideas you can use:

Who holds him captive? Why?

How long has he been there?

Does he try to communicate with the outside world? If yes, how? If not, why not?

Does he try to escape? If yes, what happens?

HORROR WRITING PROMPT #24

During a night's stay, the character discovers that the otherwise reputable hotel harbours something nasty.

Ideas you can use:

Does the guest overhear voices? If so, from where? In the reception, the restaurant, the lift (elevator), along the corridor, an adjacent room? Maybe they come from everywhere? Or she hears a voice in an out-of-bounds area. Does she hear a murder or attempted murder?

Does the character pass a door that's ajar and observe something she should not see?

What is the hotel's secret? Are guests kidnapped/murdered? Do they suddenly go missing? Or does the main character see changes in behaviour with the other guests/staff? They could suddenly act drugged, confused, mesmerised, or even possessed.

How do the staff act? Are they normal or do they act shifty? Is something slightly off-key with everything in the hotel, including décor and food?

HORROR WRITING PROMPT #25

These hands hold a human heart. Why?

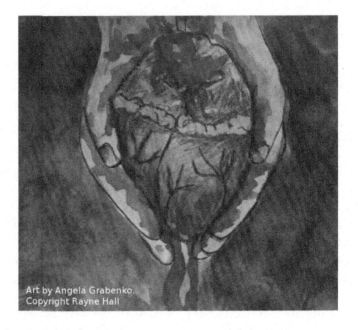

Art by Angela Grabenko.
Copyright Rayne Hall

Ideas you can use:

Is this part of a human sacrifice or a religious ritual?

Whose heart is this? How did this person die? Was she alive when the heart was cut from her body?

You can write from the perspective of the person holding the heart, or an onlooker's Point-of-View. What is this character's connection with the sacrificed person? What is his role in the ritual?

Use sensory descriptions in the story – sounds, smells, the sensation of touch.

HORROR WRITING PROMPT #26

When an inconsiderately parked car is towed away, something is discovered.

Ideas you can use:

What's underneath the car? Is it the owner's body and what was the cause of death? Are there unusual markings on the road? Satanic, perhaps?

Maybe something is found inside the car after it's taken to the compound. Is it money, and the tow-truck driver keeps it? Perhaps the ghost of the owner haunts them because of it.

Is there something in the boot (trunk)? A dead body, a weapon, an artefact or magical item, or the remains of an animal/creature/monster?

HORROR WRITING PROMPT #27

Why is this man watching the couple?

Art Jun-Pierre Shiozawa. Copyright Rayne Hall

Ideas you can use:

Who is he? Does he know the couple? What does he want from them?

Is he a serial killer, an ex-lover, a stalker, a peeping tom? What if he's someone they unwittingly harmed in the past, and now he's obsessed with vengeance? What does he plan to do to them?

What are they watching on television?

What's the first thing they notice about being observed – a sound? A moment-long reflection in the mirror? Simply a spidery feeling of being watched? How do they react to it?

Which of the two is the first to realise that something is wrong?

In this case, focus on suspense. Let the sense of danger build gradually, then escalate.

HORROR WRITING PROMPT #28

Peculiar pipes/rusted conduits are discovered in the basement of a house/skyscraper. They are in fact arteries of a sleeping creature.

Ideas you can use:

Are they discovered by a plumber or the new house-owner? The story could have a scene where blood flows from plugholes and broken pipes. Perhaps the whole building is in fact the creature. This could work well for a flash fiction piece or a short story.

HORROR WRITING PROMPT #29

This girl can harm others with her thoughts. How does she do it?

Art by Angela Grabenko.
Copyright Rayne Hall

Ideas you can use:

Does she visualise the suffering she wants to inflict? Does she mentally recite a certain spell?

Whom does she want to harm? Does she act on the spur of the moment – whenever someone has annoyed her – or does she carefully prepare a long-term campaign?

Does anyone suspect her?

Are there others with this skill, or is she the only one?

You can write this story from any Point-of-View you like – a victim's, an observer's, or even the creepy girl's.

HORROR WRITING PROMPT #30

The character touches something and a finger or even the entire hand swells.

Ideas you can use:

Does it happen while gardening or cutting vegetables, or a do-it-yourself project or during house renovations?

This could be a slow-build kind of story, where the character notices something weird and has to backtrack to discover what caused the swelling. All the while it becomes infected, or becomes a serious wound.

Is the swelling actually eggs beneath the skin? Did the character unearth an alien/ancient artefact, or disturb a creature's/insect's nest?

HORROR WRITING PROMPT #31

A ghost looks out through this window. At whom, and why?

Photo by Rayne Hall (copyright)

Ideas you can use:

Who is the ghost? Did it use to live in this house? Why does it haunt? What does it need?

Who sees the ghost? Perhaps the house opposite this derelict building is inhabited, and someone who lives there feels observed. Or maybe a character walks past this house every day on the way home from work, and always sees this ghost.

Does the ghost try to communicate with the living human character? How?

Ghost stories work best if both the ghost and the living human have important needs that are somehow related. Perhaps they are similar needs, or the direct opposite.

What if the ghost wants to warn the living human? Perhaps the ghost once made a devastating mistake (one that ultimately led to her inability to find rest), and now she sees a living woman about to make the bad choice. How does she present her warning? Can she speak? Does the living human listen?

This story may lend itself to an element of romance – either in the ghost's backstory, or in the story of the living character.

HORROR WRITING PROMPT #32

A farmer/hiker/driver discovers a field with a strange smoke or gas coming from the churned soil.

Ideas you can use:

Something is buried or has crash-landed. Are the fumes toxic? When inhaled, does it make the character insane or become a murderer? Does it possess them?

Is it a creature buried underground and has suddenly woken? If so, why now? Was its slumber disturbed by the character? Or is it a cycle of every one-hundred years?

Farmer: if it is smoke, the farmer would first think of vandals. Does he dismiss it and later in the season grow crops which then infect the population (apocalyptic novel)? Or does he knowingly sell the produce (short story)?

Hiker: is the character lost? Does he fall and hurt himself? Does he use the route as a short cut and unknowingly disturb the ground?

Driver: the driver pulls up for a photograph, or maybe has an accident. If it is an accident, is it because he inhales the vapour? Or perhaps somebody or something ran out in front of his car.

HORROR WRITING PROMPT #33

What is this person after?

Art by Angela Grabenko.
Copyright Rayne Hall

Ideas you can use:

Who is he? A living human (perhaps a prisoner, or a desperate homeless beggar), a zombie, a ghost, a vampire, or something else altogether?

What does he want?

Is he looking out from inside a house, or from the outside in? At what?

What stops him from entering (or leaving) the building?

HORROR WRITING PROMPT #34

The character takes a bite out of a burger/donut/sandwich and sees rot/mould/insects.

Ideas you can use:

This would be great for a flash fiction piece, or perhaps used as a scene in a novel or short story. You can have the character bite into any type of everyday food or treat, but be sure to make the reader *taste* how foul it is.

Is the food actually rotten/mouldy, or is the character hallucinating? Are there really insects, or is it the character's imagination because of a phobia? When the character bites into the food, does he feel guilt (perhaps he's on a diet and shouldn't eat ice cream), pain (the apple pie is extremely hot), or regret (it's the last cookie in the packet)? Does it taste bitter because he has in fact poisoned himself (suicide?) Or has someone else poisoned him? Who is the suspect?

Or is it human meat that is eaten? And does he realise this? The character could be enjoying it, and the twist being that it's actually their own flesh. Again, this would be perfect for a flash fiction story.

HORROR WRITING PROMPT #35

What triggered the rising of the zombies in this picture?

Ideas you can use:

Does the full moon make the zombies rise from their graves? If yes, why has this not happened when the moon was full before?

Has a human raised the zombies? If yes, what for? Is he watching them now?

What is the zombies' immediate need after rising from their graves? Are they seeking sustenance, or are they looking to orient themselves, or do they want to reunite with loved ones?

With this story, you have several options for the Point-of-View. You can choose the PoV of the magician who raises the zombies, of the opponent who tries to prevent the raising, an observer, a victim, or even a zombie.

HORROR WRITING PROMPT #36

In a conservation or nature reserve, the animals aren't the typical creatures found in such places.

Ideas you can use:

In a novel, the conservation area could be at the core of the plot. To begin with, you could make the reader assume they are normal animals... Until something goes wrong.

Perhaps the main character is a police detective, unravelling the mystery behind the animals themselves. Or is the main character the creator herself? Maybe the animals are in fact bloodthirsty monsters?

You can weave in the perspectives of visitors and delivery drivers who get caught up in whatever chaos unfolds.

What if people get kidnapped? Or maybe they are accidentally killed and the creator is torn between science and conscience. Maybe the victims have their blood infused with that of the animals, and ultimately become the animals/creatures. Are they stitched abominations, assembled from parts of different creatures, like in the classic novels *Frankenstein* or *The Island of Dr Moreau*? Remember that those books were written and published long ago. A modern tale will need to consider modern scientific knowledge in order to be plausible.

HORROR WRITING PROMPT #37

What kind of magic does this woman work? Does it go to plan?

Art by Angela Grabenko.
Copyright Rayne Hall

Ideas you can use:

Is she levitating a ball, conjuring a sphere of light, or gazing into the orb to see the future?

What kind of ritual does she use to achieve this?

Although she initiated the magic, she is clearly shocked. What's happening? Does she see something that frightens her?

What if she discovers that a powerful evil entity has become involved in her supposedly innocent spell?

What if she sees something devastating about her own future?

What if she realises that she won't be able to end or undo the spell, because the portal has closed?

HORROR WRITING PROMPT #38

A woodsman carves a mythical creature and it comes alive.

Ideas you can use:

Put a twist on the classic *Pinocchio* story and crank up the horror factor. How does this happen? Was the felled tree sacred and so this creature takes revenge? Does the woodsman know what he's carving, or does he become mesmerised/hypnotised? Perhaps he creates more than one creature and every one of them becomes animated.

Do these animals/creatures end up mating with the local fauna? From there, you could have them run amok through the woodland, and eventually into an urban setting. Imagine the fun you could have as everyday life in suburbia becomes a hunting ground for these creatures.

Maybe our woodsman carves organs/body parts. Are these carvings used for prosthetic limbs, and do the people who now have them begin to act oddly? Is this a story about tree spirits possessing the locals? Do they avenge the recent felling of trees to make way for a new town?

HORROR WRITING PROMPT #39

Why is this person crawling in this hallway?

Art by Jun-Pierre Shiozawa. Copyright Rayne Hall

Ideas you can use:

What is this institution? A hospital? A prison? A lunatic asylum? A high-tech torture dungeon? A research station for medical experiments on humans?

Does it officially serve this purpose, or is it supposedly something else, and nobody must know what really goes on inside?

Who is the person? A prisoner? A patient?

What is he escaping from?

Why is he crawling, not walking or running? Has the 'treatment' destroyed his ability to walk or his sense of balance? What other impairments does he suffer?

Is he the only victim, or are there others? Are the others also trying to escape?

What if this is not an attempt at escape, but part of a rebellion or major act of vengeance?

Who is the story's Point-of-View character? You can use the perspective of the crawling person, a warden, a doctor/torturer/scientist, or a visitor who realises for the first time that this institution is not what it seems to be.

HORROR WRITING PROMPT #40

A character receives an invitation/leaflet to attend a new local yoga/ Pilates/karate class, and she decides to go. When she arrives, everyone in the room is simply standing on a mat doing absolutely nothing.

Ideas you can use:

This would work well for a short story. When the character joins in, does she fall into a trance with the others? Are participants drugged somehow? From the watercooler perhaps, or is it some kind of gas pumped into the room? Is this a peculiar sect, and when the character goes home, does she try to convert her family or act out some other command?

HORROR WRITING PROMPT #41

Write about this ritual.

Art by Angela Grabenko.
Copyright Rayne Hall

Ideas you can use:

What is going on here? Is the baby being baptised or sacrificed?

The crosses seem to indicate that the ritual is connected to the Christian faith – but some things are distinctly odd. Is this a cult?

Who is the person holding the baby? Is it the mother? A priest? Why is she veiled? Does she not want to be recognised?

Who are the others?

Who brought the baby to the ritual? The parents? Strangers? Are they present?

Why did they bring the baby? Did they assume this was a legitimate church and a regular baptism, and realise too late what was going on? Or did they surrender the baby to buy their own lives?

What if the main character's own baby is to be sacrificed unless she provides another living child as a substitute?

HORROR WRITING PROMPT #42

A character purchases something from a market/boot fair/garage sale.

Ideas you can use:

Perhaps the character is a collector and discovers a rare item. Or maybe she's simply drawn to the object because of its attractiveness, yet there's something which later haunts her. Is it a trinket and something happens to/possesses the wearer?

The item could be stolen. Does she recognise that it's the object her relative/deceased relative used to own? Or did the item once belong to the character herself?

Whatever the item's nature, the main character could become obsessed with it.

HORROR WRITING PROMPT #43

Why are the door and window of this house bricked up – to keep something or someone out... or to keep someone or something in?

Photo by Rayne Hall (copyright)

Ideas you can use:

Are the owners trying to keep out humans, or wild animals, or paranormal entities? Are they successful? What will happen if the menace gets in?

What if they keep someone inside? Whom – a prisoner, a lunatic relative, a dangerous animal? Why must this creature not get out?

Does the house have other doors, or is this the only way in and out?

Do other people in the neighbourhood know what's going on? Have they, too, bricked up their homes?

What if the creature/menace/prisoner does get in or out?

You can tell the story from the PoV of the house owner, the prisoner or the neighbour.

HORROR WRITING PROMPT #44

A pet brings home an unusual creature.

Ideas you can use:

A cat/dog finds the creature and brings it home. Is the creature now left in the garden or roaming indoors? Does the owner know immediately or are there droppings/scratches/fur left around the house? Does the owner live alone or have a family? How does this new creature affect everyone involved?

Perhaps it's an alien/mutant/hybrid but whatever it is, the creature is something the owner has never before seen. Think of the repercussions if the pet eats the creature, or even mates with it. Does the pet sadly die and is the body found being eaten by a neighbour's pet? And so the cycle continues…

You can give your story authenticity if you write about the kind of pet you're familiar with. For example, as a cat owner, you'll be able to describe believably how a cat behaves with a new catch.

HORROR WRITING PROMPT #45

The character wakes up in a strange place where he definitely should not be.

Ideas you can use:

Does he wake up in the central reservation of the motorway/highway, or in the middle of a sport or school field, or on board a train/bus/plane? Maybe it's even on private property.

Perhaps he is handcuffed or naked. Maybe he's covered in blood (his own or someone else's), or in possession of an unusual weapon/secret documents/an old or unusual key/item.

This kind of story does not have to be written from the character's point of view. Think of a kind-hearted driver who pulls over, an early-morning athlete, or a fellow passenger.

HORROR WRITING PROMPT #46

Write about this bird in a cemetery.

Art by Angela Grabenko.
Copyright Rayne Hall

Ideas you can use:

Is it night, dusk or dawn?

Is this a bird of prey that always hunts at night or at twilight? Perhaps it is getting ready to hunt. Why does it hunt in a cemetery? What kind of prey is it after?

What if it's not about to hunt, but has been woken? By what? Is it alerting other creatures of the danger?

It's obviously making a sound. Describe that sound. What is it communicating, and to whom? A warning? A mating call? A call of distress? An assertion of its territory?

Perhaps the bird is the 'familiar' of a magician. If so, where is the magician, and what is he doing at night in the cemetery?

HORROR WRITING PROMPT #47

Something floats under a bridge.

Ideas you can use:

Is it a body, a boat wreck, or furniture? It could be a bed with someone tied to it, and the body has a stake through its heart.

Where does the main character stand where he sees the floating object? On the bridge? Beneath it? Why is he there?

Does he recognise the floating object? Is it the person they were looking for, or the boat that they were supposed to buy? Or could it be their bed with a lover tied to it?

What does he do – does he let the object drift on, or does he try to pull it out of the water?

Does our character feel guilt, relief, or confusion? What if he is the reason behind it floating along the river? Does he witness someone pull it from the water and if so, what story could unfold from there?

HORROR WRITING PROMPT #48

Write about this character. What happened to her? Why is she walking there? What does she seek?

Art by Jun-Pierre Shiozawa.
Copyright Rayne Hall.

Ideas you can use:

Has she been kidnapped, raped, tortured? By whom and for how long? Has she escaped?

What if she isn't a living human, but a vampire or a ghost?

What does she want? Why is she walking there?

You can write the story from the PoV of this woman, or from the PoV of a character who encounters her.

The encounter can be the beginning, the middle or the end of the story.

HORROR WRITING PROMPT #49

A car park attendant/refuse collector witnesses or discovers something illegal/horrific.

Ideas you can use:

Does he see or overhear something which puts him in danger? Does he witness an exchange of money/drugs, a heated argument, a fight or even a murder? Perhaps he finds an abandoned car or something in the waste bin/trash can? Is there a dead body inside? Or a severed limb? Or a head… which talks?

Is the car the one he sold the week before, or does he know these people? Is it the character's boss or work colleague? Should he report the incident/discovery, or will it put the character's job in jeopardy?

HORROR WRITING PROMPT #50

Write about this character.

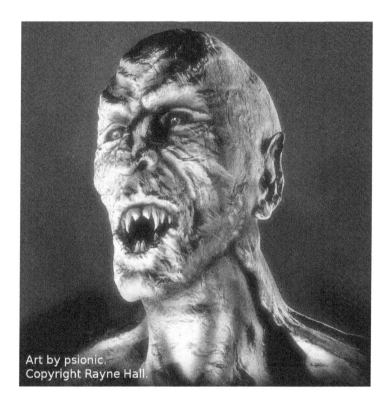

Art by psionic.
Copyright Rayne Hall.

Ideas you can use:

Is he alive, dead, or something in between, a zombie perhaps?

How did he get to this state? How did he become disfigured? What caused his pointed teeth – did he have them filed like this, or did someone else do it, or did they change shape when he died?

What does he want or need right now? Why is this need so urgent?

HORROR WRITING PROMPT #51

A character returns to a coffee shop to collect a coat and finds something in the pocket.

Ideas you can use:

Is it a wallet containing a heap of cash, with an address? Is it a car key with a devil's face on the fob? Drugs? A message? A severed finger?

The story may focus around the dilemma of tracking down the owner/culprit.

Is the object magical and does it make the character hear voices? Or maybe even possess her? Does it lead her to an ex-lover or family member? Or someone who's stalking her? Does it lure her to her death? How does she overcome it?

HORROR WRITING PROMPT #52

What is happening here?

Art by Angela Grabenko.
Copyright Rayne Hall

Ideas you can use:

Who is the standing creature – an abusive parent or husband? A zombie? A serial killer?

When and how does she become aware of the danger?

Is she sleeping in her familiar bed, or somewhere else – in a friend's home or in a hotel, perhaps?

HORROR WRITING PROMPT #53

During the night, a character goes to the kitchen for a drink of water and sees something outside, glinting beneath the moonlight or huddling in the shadow.

Ideas you can use:

Where is this 'something' – in the garden (yard) or in the street?

Is it a ghost or ghoul, or a package or even a crate?

The character could be a wife who sees the apparition of her dead husband, or a husband who sees the undead corpse of his recently deceased wife? It could be the ghost of a hit-and-run incident earlier that day, in which the main character believes they're hallucinating due to guilt.

If the object is a crate or package, what does it contain? A body/ bodies or body parts? Again, it could be something to do with a recent tragedy.

HORROR WRITING PROMPT #54

Why are these stickmen hanging from the trees?

Art Jun-Pierre Shiozawa.
Copyright Rayne Hall

Ideas you can use:

Are these part of a ritual or a magic spell?

Are they intended to avert harm from the people who live in the house, or to bring harm to an enemy?

Who hung them there – the people living in the house, or someone who hates the house's inhabitants?

Who is supposed to see these stickmen? Who is supposed not to see them?

Have they been hung up permanently, or only for one night?

What effect do the stickmen – or the ritual/spell – have?

HORROR WRITING PROMPT #55

Determined to get answers, a character smashes open a shed padlock.

Ideas you can use:

Are we in a quiet rural area or a busy urban setting where the neighbours could overlook?

Who put the padlock there? Does our character do this during the night or day, and is he sneaky about it? Is it his own house, or a neighbour's? This would work well for a short story where the plot revolves around the mystery.

Whatever is revealed beyond the door could lead the character to question her family or spouse. Is there evidence of experiments or kidnapping, or does it force the character to face a fear? Does it bring back childhood memories and make her confront a family member?

HORROR WRITING PROMPT #56

A character gets fed up with gifts being left on her doorstep.

Ideas you can use:

Is it a box of chocolates, flowers or alcohol? Could they be animal sacrifices left by a pet or by something more sinister? Does the character catch someone in the act and demand answers?

If it's chocolate, then is there a stalker involved? If it is a bunch of flowers, perhaps the twist could be that our main character is dead (great for flash fiction).

Perhaps the gifts left on her doorstep make her step outside in bare feet. What could the outcome of that be? Does she step on broken glass from a wine bottle?

While she is outside, does this allow the culprit to sneak indoors?

HORROR WRITING PROMPT #57

Write about the ghost haunting this house.

Copyright Rayne Hall

Ideas you can use:

Who is haunting? Why? Perhaps the ghost needs to conclude an important matter before he finds rest. What might this matter be? Does he need to atone for an evil deed, reveal the location of a treasure, expose a dark secret, win a woman's love?

Why is he haunting this house? Did he live, die or commit a crime here?

Where exactly does he haunt? Choose the room. What time of the day or night does he appear? Are these manifestations regular – for example, every night or only during the new moon? Or do specific conditions – such as pretty female houseguests or noisy parties – attract his visits?

Now think of a human who encounters this ghost. Does she live there or visit? Perhaps she's a lodger or a foreign student who has rented a room while attending the local college.

In what ways do the ghost's and the living human's stories mesh? What happens when they meet?

HORROR WRITING PROMPT #58

A character returns home to find something on his living-room carpet.

Ideas you can use:

Is the window broken, and on the carpet is there a rock with a message tied to it? A threatening note or racial hatred? What if there are no signs of breakages or a break-in? Does this suggest someone left it there who had legitimate access to the place? Perhaps a spouse or an ex-lover?

Maybe something has burst up through the floorboards.

What if the character discovers a dead neighbour, an intruder with a bizarre fatal wound?

Perhaps what he finds poses a threat to his life, or the lives of his loved ones.

Maybe he doesn't want anyone else to see this. Why not? To what lengths will he go to conceal it?

HORROR WRITING PROMPT #59

A mechanic/plumber/handyman discovers an unusual wire/pipe which doesn't belong to the vehicle/appliance.

Ideas you can use:

When he detaches the wire/pipe, what happens? Does it wound the character or someone else? Does it make him see things? Does it infect him?

How did it get there?

Without that part, does the vehicle drive differently/dangerously, does the appliance act in a peculiar way or do something completely out of the ordinary?

How does this affect the owner or family members?

Who originally put that part there and for what purpose?

HORROR WRITING PROMPT #60

The full moon illuminates a spooky scene. Write the story from the PoV of a person who comes across this scene and at first can't quite see what – if anything – is happening.

Art by Jun-Pierre Shiozawa.
Copyright Rayne Hall.

Ideas you can use:

The white object in the centre appears to be a human body. Is this person sleeping? Why does she sleep in this place? Or is she dead – and if so, how did she die? If she was murdered or sacrificed, is her killer still around?

What the PoV character realises that this is a human body, how does he respond? Does he try to get closer, to wake the sleeper, to check that she's okay, or to take a closer look at the naked beauty? Or does he flee, in case the killer is hanging around?

HORROR WRITING PROMPT #61

Suddenly the lights go out.

Ideas you can use:

This could be a pivotal scene in your novel, or the opening scene in a short story or flash fiction piece. Does it happen in a theatre or cinema, or perhaps at a fairground, amusement arcade, a shop or shopping mall?

Where would be the worse place for this to happen to your character? Then, in the darkness, what would happen? Is there a killing, an abduction, or does a portal to the netherworld open and snatch up a character?

HORROR WRITING PROMPT #62

Something bad happens to a character who returns to a hotel room after a business meeting.

Ideas you can use:

Is there a decapitated head on the bedside table/nightstand? Does the character hear its voice even though the dead lips do not move? Or does it in fact speak through dead lips?

Does she see a ghost, or is someone already in the room and asleep on the bed? Is there a murder weapon?

Has her client drugged her, intending to harm her?

For this, try to face your *own* fear. What's the most terrible thing you can imagine happening to you in your hotel room at midnight?

What if the hotel owners are not your typical business-minded people?

HORROR WRITING PROMPT #63

Who wears this mask, and for what purpose?

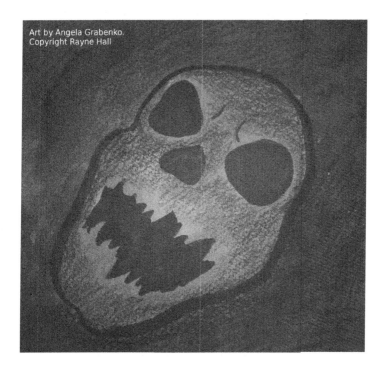

Art by Angela Grabenko.
Copyright Rayne Hall

Ideas you can use:

Does the killer wear the mask so he can't be recognised by witnesses?

Does the torturer force his victim to wear the mask?

Is the mask part of a ritual, or perhaps of an erotic game that goes wrong?

What if a zombie wears the mask to hide the decaying flesh of his true face?

HORROR WRITING PROMPT #64

The character drives through a town and witnesses a crime.

Ideas you can use:

Are we in a rural setting or urban, a familiar town/hometown of the character?

Is he a tourist or businessman, or is he heading back after a long time away from family?

What crime does he witness: a murder/car theft/bank robbery?

How does he get tangled up with it? What if he gets wounded in the shooting? What if he gets framed for the crime?

Is he alone in the vehicle? Perhaps his passenger goes missing, or gets implicated or involved in the crime.

HORROR WRITING PROMPT #65

Two characters are walking together, and something falls from the sky.

Ideas you can use:

What is the object? Perhaps someone threw it at them? Is it something that has broken off from a plane or balloon overhead, or an aircraft? Maybe it is deliberately dropped from a drone.

Whatever it is, does it seriously injure or even kill one of the characters?

This could work well for any length story. Whether a sharp punchy flash fiction piece or a short story, this scene could be the main plot point. For a novel, it could be a pivotal moment where it forces a character to act, or even maim him to forever change his life.

HORROR WRITING PROMPT #66

The people who lived here had dreams of happiness. What destroyed their dreams and their home?

Ideas you can use:

Were they newlyweds? A young family? A newly retired couple? Expatriates?

What caused the problem? What made them leave their home? Evil neighbours? War? An infectious plague? A toxic cloud? A horde of flesh-eating zombies? An earthquake? Sickness? Disability? Poverty? Religious mania? Political persecution? Paranoia?

Describe what their life was like before the disaster struck, and what hopes they had for the future.

Did they leave immediately, or did they desperately try to stick it out until no hope was left?

HORROR WRITING PROMPT #67

A character is trapped in a room with a gun and one round of ammunition.

Ideas you can use:

Why is he in there? Who is he? What's his motivation? Is he wounded? Is there someone else in the room? Perhaps there's a dead body slumped in a chair. There's an empty shell beside the body, and it's apparent that the person has used the gun on himself.

What will the character do? For how long will he hold out?

Are people watching? Is the character innocent or guilty of something against the captors? This could be an emotionally driven flash fiction piece or short story.

HORROR WRITING PROMPT #68

A character gets threatened in a nightclub.

Ideas you can use:

Does the confrontation escalate in the club or outside? Has someone followed the character into the club?

Is it a date gone wrong, or did the character flirt with the wrong woman? Is it a club where the character was not invited? Is he underage, illegally drinking, or selling drugs? Is it a 'members only' or high society club?

Think of occasions when you visited a pub or club. Recall the atmosphere, the layout of the place, the events, and any confusions or embarrassments you experienced. What could possibly happen to you in such a place that would turn your life upside down? Put your character into that situation and crank up the confrontational/ horror factor.

HORROR WRITING PROMPT #69

A character needs to use the toilet/restroom in a town where he's never been before. She just makes it to the public toilet building – and finds that this is shut and has been out of use for a long time. The need is urgent. What does she do? Where does she go?

Ideas you can use:

Recall a situation when you really, really needed to use a toilet. How did it feel? What did you do?

Describe the physical sensation of a pressing full bladder. This description may not need to be long, but it should be graphic, so the readers remember their own experiences vividly.

This character needs to relieve herself urgently. Perhaps she has tried several options – a nearby coffee shop is closed, at the hotel she's refused entry – and she's getting desperate. Does she seek privacy in a dark alleyway? Or does she accept the invitation of a stranger to use his bathroom?

After emptying her bladder, she feels better... and immediately realises that she has made a mistake. What's the first thing she sees that makes her aware of the danger? Perhaps the stranger comes at her with a big blade. Or maybe she hears the key turn, locking the toilet from the outside. What if she finds something grisly in the bathroom?

You may want to use a female character for this story, because a woman can't relieve herself discreetly without disrobing. This makes the situation more urgent and embarrassing.

HORROR WRITING PROMPT #70

The character's partner/sibling/parent fails to return indoors after putting out the rubbish (garbage).

Ideas you can use:

After his family member vanishes, the character goes to investigate. What does he see? Perhaps the bins are overturned, or there's a kidnap/suicide note, or a weapon, or stack of money? Maybe there are footprints or even blood, or maybe he witnesses a fight/abduction/murder/suicide.

How would witnessing such a thing change the character's life from that moment?

HORROR WRITING PROMPT #71

Instead of taking his passenger directly to the requested destination, a taxi driver stops somewhere to do something else. Then he continues the journey, without giving an explanation.

Ideas you can use:

Perhaps the story takes place in a foreign country where the character speaks the language only a little or not at all. Perhaps the lack of a common language is the reason the driver doesn't explain. Does the passenger attempt to ask? If yes, how does the driver respond?

Perhaps the driver stops off somewhere questionable to pick up a package. Is the package placed (delicately) or thrown (carelessly) into the boot/trunk?

Maybe the driver meets someone. Do they have a heated discussion or even argument? Do they whisper, gesture dramatically, or shake hands over an apparent deal?

What if the driver takes another passenger on board? Is this someone the driver obviously knows well, or someone he seems to fear?

Is the location where they stop secluded, urban, rural, creepy, or fairly out in the open?

What if the driver locks the car from the outside while he picks up the package or conducts the meeting?

Perhaps the character doesn't see much (it could be dark), but he hears the voices from the meeting – or perhaps he hears a gunshot or a scream.

Perhaps he hears nothing ominous during the stop, but later, hears noises from the taxi's boot/trunk.

HORROR WRITING PROMPT #72

Every town has a 'crazy' person: it's the woman who pushes the pram/pushchair that contains a doll or teddy bear; it's the old man who wanders along the pavement, muttering; it's the tramp/hobo who huddles in a shop doorway you always pass on the way to work. Write about a town's crazy person.

Ideas you can use:

What would happen if someone mean/drunk/on a dare snatches the doll from the woman's pram?

How does the muttering man retaliate when someone asks him for directions?

Does the doorway vagrant sleepwalk, or suddenly attack a passer-by?

HORROR WRITING PROMPT #73

It's the character's first day of their new job, and she experiences something unexpected.

Ideas you can use:

Does she see a colleague steal something, or do something questionable/illegal? If it's an office job, perhaps there are sticky-notes left everywhere. Are they crude? Do they reveal secrets? Do they contain warnings of why the character should not work there?

It could be in a factory where there's graffiti scribbled around the shelving or on stock. Perhaps there's bullying and the character gets caught up with that, whether as a victim or a witness. Maybe the character sees the ghost of someone who was murdered in the building. Or perhaps it's the ghost of someone who was bullied and so committed suicide.

Think of your own previous jobs or even your current occupation. The old adage is "write what you know" and so this could be something close to your heart. Have you ever seen anything untoward? Indeed, have you ever done anything at work you're not proud of and hoped no one ever finds out? Could you write a horror story from a personal experience?

HORROR WRITING PROMPT #74

A sleeping character wakes from a noise under her bed. When she looks, she discovers something terrifying.

Art by Angela Grabenko.
Copyright Rayne Hall

Ideas you can use:

What is under her bed? A person? An animal? A bloody weapon? A mass of creepy crawlies?

Is it really there, or is she hallucinating?

Describe the noise she hears. How does she react to it? If she was asleep, her subconscious may have incorporated the noise into a dream. Then she woke up, and the noise continued or recurred.

Is she frightened by the noise, or only by what she sees?

How did the thing get under her bed? Was it there before the character went to sleep, or did it arrive later? Why is it under her bed, and not in another part of the room or under someone else's bed?

What does the character do?

You may find it helpful to remember occasions from your childhood when you feared a monster under your bed. If you had such fears as a child, recall them vividly, and use them for this story.

HORROR WRITING PROMPT #75

Look behind you. What do you see? Imagine that this object or person is malevolent.

Ideas you can use:

Use whatever item or person you see – especially if it's obviously harmless – and use your twisted imagination to make it evil. That pretty dried-flower arrangement, the ornamental mirror, the two old ladies chatting on the bus, yesterday's discarded clothes you haven't tidied away yet... anything can take on life and become dangerous.

What does this object or person do? Why?

Start with a small clue to the item's malevolence, build the danger gradually, and let it escalate.

HORROR WRITING PROMPT #76

What annoyed you today? Exaggerate that irritation so it because a cause for unstoppable fury. Imagine what a character might do.

Ideas you can use:

Really use something that annoyed you today. It can be a tiny irritation ~ perhaps a mosquito buzzing in the room, a stupid advertising jingle, a dripping water tap, a flatmate who didn't wash up his breakfast dishes, your neighbour's noisy lawnmower – or something that has infuriated you for a while – the way your boss overloads you with work and never shows any appreciation, your boyfriend's repeated cheating and lying, the coyote that has killed your beloved pet cat, the contemptuous way your son-in-law treats your daughter.

Magnify the trigger and the emotion. Let the character be furious beyond rationality. Perhaps the anger builds gradually, from mild to ferocious.

You can write this from the perspective of the angry character, or from the PoV of the person who (knowingly or unwittingly) attracted the anger and becomes the target for the fury.

HORROR WRITING PROMPT #77

A character meets a demon (who may be disguised as an angel) who offers him an opportunity: He can inflict any kind of harm on anyone. Nobody will ever know about it. There is absolutely no catch, and there will be no price to pay.

Ideas you can use:

What will this character do? Will she kill a dictator, take revenge on someone who harmed her, punish the people who turned her down for a job or an acting role? Will she eliminate a love rival or a business competitor? Will she strike her cheating husband with impotence, or torment her childhood abuser with endless nightmares?

With absolutely no consequences, what (moral or ethical) boundaries will she push or step over?

You may want to look into your own darkest desires. Remember the people who harmed you or your loved ones. If you could punish them without fear of consequences, what would you do and how far would you go?

This is not a traditional 'deal with the devil' tale where there is a price to pay. In this story, the horror stems from the fact that there will be no price to pay, no consequences whatsoever, so the character is free to inflict whatever cruelty she wishes. The only thing that may hold her back is her own conscience... and that may not stand up to temptation for long.

DEAR READER,

Mark and I hope you found these prompts inspiring, and that you had fun playing with the ideas.

Remember: the prompts are just the seeds. It's up to you to nurture and grow them into flourishing plants, and the resulting stories are yours alone.

We'd be delighted if you post a review on Amazon or some other book site where you have an account and posting privileges. Maybe you can mention what kind of horror fiction you write, and even mention which of the prompts are your favourites.

Email me the link to your review, and I'll send you a free review copy (ebook) of one of my other Writer's Craft books. Let me know which one you would like: Writing Fight Scenes, Writing Scary Scenes, The Word-Loss Diet, Writing About Magic, Writing About Villains, Writing Dark Stories, Euphonics For Writers, Writing Short Stories to Promote Your Novels, Twitter for Writers, Why Does My Book Not Sell? 20 Simple Fixes, Writing Vivid Settings, How To Train Your Cat To Promote Your Book, Writing Deep Point of View, Getting Book Reviews, Novel Revision Prompts, Writing Vivid Dialogue, Writing Vivid Characters, Writing Book Blurbs and Synopses, Writing Vivid Plots, Write Your Way Out Of Depression: Practical Self-Therapy For Creative Writers, Fantasy Writing Prompts, Horror Writing Prompts, Dr Rayne's Guide to Writerly Disorders, Writing Love Scenes, How To Write That Scene. The series is growing fast. You can see all the books on this page on my website: http://www.raynehall.com/books-for-writers.

At the end of this book, I'm attaching an excerpt from Writing Scary Scenes, so you can experience the style of my guides, and see if it's right for you.

My email is <u>contact@raynehall.com</u>. Drop me a line if you've spotted any typos which have escaped the proof-reader's eagle eyes, or want to give me private feedback or have questions.

You can also contact me on Twitter: <u>https://twitter.com/RayneHall</u>. Tweet me that you've read this book, and I'll probably follow you back.

If you find this book helpful, it would be great if you could spread the word about it. Maybe you know other practising or aspiring horror writers who would benefit.

With best wishes for your writing success,

Rayne Hall

ACKNOWLEDGEMENTS

I give sincere thanks to the beta readers and critiquers who read the draft and offered valuable feedback: Linda Hullinger, Jim aka the.release.101, Stephanie Lay, and everyone else who chimed in with feedback and suggestions.

The book cover is by Erica Syverson and Manuel Berbin. Julia Gibbs proof-read the manuscript, and Eled Cernik formatted the book.

And finally, I say thank you to my cats Sulu and Uhura (Yura for short) who took turns snuggling on the desk between my arms and watching me type. They're delightful, well-behaved muses. I also thank my third cat, ginger Janice, for not disrupting my writing as much as usual.

Rayne Hall

EXCERPT FROM
WRITING SCARY SCENES
BY RAYNE HALL

CHAPTER 8

DARK AND DANGEROUS

Do you want your readers to fear for your heroine's safety? Here's a simple technique on how to make a scene seriously frightening:

Turn the lights off.

Darkness makes people nervous, and everything is much more frightening in the dark. Can you change the time or location of your scene so it happens in darkness? The darker, the better. Absolute darkness is the scariest, when the protagonist sees nothing at all and has to grope to find her way. However, partial darkness can be spooky, too, especially with flickering lights and shadows.

Some ideas for darkness

A windowless room

Night time

Drawn curtains

A power-cut

Fuel shortage

Energy conservation

Candles burn out

Wind blows candle

Lantern falls into abyss

Bullet shatters light-bulb

Canopy of trees blocks out the sun

New moon

Clouds veil the moon

Solar eclipse

Thick smoke

Sandstorm

Lights turned off for love-making

Deep cave

Hiding in a dark closet

Flash-light battery dies

If the storyline permits, let the darkness increase gradually:

Dusk gives way to night

The camp-fire burns down

Clouds thicken

USING THE SENSES

In the dark, humans are deprived of the sense on which they rely most: seeing. Other senses sharpen, especially hearing. Your point-of-view character suddenly hears a lot more noises. These sounds add to the scary effect. In Chapter 5 *Sounds Build Suspense* we'll explore how to make the most of sounds.

If the darkness is absolute, the PoV character relies on her sense of touch as she gropes her way around. Describe how the walls, the furniture, the trees feel to her fingers, and how the ground feels underfoot. Smells also become more noticeable in the dark, and you can give the reader an intense experience by mentioning a smell or two.

Darkness often brings low temperatures. Chills can increase the scare factor, so mention the cool breeze brushing your heroine's arms, the cellar's icy stone walls, the cold water dripping from the ceiling of the cave, the cold seeping through the thin soles of her shoes.

EXAMPLES FROM BOOKS

Lynda La Plante: *Cold Shoulder*

It was dark, the alley lit only by neon flashes from the main street; not a single bulb above the many exit doors leading into it remained intact.

Dean Koontz: *The Bad Place*

The apartment was a well of shadows, oil-black and pooled deep. Faint ash-gray light outlined the windows but provided no illumination to the room.

GRR Martin: *Only Kids are Afraid of the Dark*

No moonlight sifted down; no stars shone from above; only night, sinister and eternal, and the swirling, chocking gray mist that shifted and stirred with every movement.

Ramsey Campbell: *Heading Home*

When the flame steadies you can see darkness gaping for inches around the laboratory door.

Angela Carter: *The Lady of the House of Love*

Although it was not yet dark outside, the curtains were closely drawn and only the sparing light trickling from a single oil lamp showed him how dismal his surroundings were.

Tanith Lee: *Wolfland*

Even with the feeble light, she could barely see ten inches before her, and felt cautiously about with her free hand, dreading to collide with ornament or furniture and thereby rouse her enemies. The stray gleams, shot back at her from a mirror or a picture frame, misled rather than aided her.

DRAWBACKS

This technique suits almost any story, whether you want to send mild shivers across the skin of the paranormal romance reader, or chill the reader's bones in a thriller. However, some scenes need daylight for the plot to work. Also, if scene after scene takes place in the dark, the reader gets so used to it that it's no longer scary.

EXCERPT FROM
WRITING SCARY SCENES

Here are two sample chapters from another Writer's Craft book, *Writing Scary Scenes,* which you may find useful.

CHAPTER 5

SOUNDS BUILD SUSPENSE

Of all the senses, the sense of hearing serves best to create excitement, suspense and fear, so use it liberally.

Mention and describe several sounds, and insert those sentences in different sections of the scene. This technique suits all stories in all genres. It works especially well if the scene is set in darkness, because the sense of hearing is sharpened when the vision is reduced.

ACTION SOUNDS

Use the sounds of the ongoing action, especially of the threat: the villain's footsteps clanking down the metal stairs, the dungeon door squealing open, the rasp of the prison guard's voice, the attack dog's growl, the rattling of the torture instruments in the tool box.

BACKGROUND SOUNDS

In addition, use the background noises which aren't connected to the action. Think about the noises of the setting.

Examples

A shutter banged against the frame.

A car door slammed. A motor whined.

A dog howled in the distance.

The motor stuttered and whined.

The ceiling fan whirred.

The wind whined.

The rope clanked rhythmically against the flagpole.

Computers beeped, phones shrilled, and printers whirred.

Waves hissed against the shore.

Waves thumped against the hull.

Thunder rumbled.

Rodent feet scurried.

Water gurgled in the drainpipe.

EXTREME SUSPENSE

A few 'sound' sentences work wonders for the atmosphere of your scary scene. You can insert them wherever it makes sense – and even in random places.

The most powerful use of this technique is to make a suspenseful moment even more suspenseful.

By inserting a sentence about an irrelevant background noise, you can slow the pace without lowering the excitement. This turns the tension and suspense up several notches.

Here's an example:

Before

The knife came closer to her throat. And closer.

She squirmed against the bonds, knowing it to be useless.

The cold edge of steel touched her skin. She tried not to swallow.

After

The knife came closer to her throat. And closer.

She squirmed against the bonds, knowing it to be useless.

Somewhere in the distance, a car door slammed and a motor whined.

The cold edge of steel touched her skin. She tried not to swallow.

COLLECTING SOUNDS

Whenever you're away from home and have a few moments to spare, listen to the noises around you. Jot them down in your writer's notebook. (If you don't have a writer's notebook yet, get one: a small lightweight one with ruled pages is practical.)

If possible, describe what the noises sound like, using verbs (*a car rattles up the road* or *a car whines up the road*)

By observing and noting the noises of one place per day (365 places per year), you can build a fantastic resource which will come in handy for future fiction projects. This is also a handy way of killing time, especially in boring meetings, at the laundrette, at the railway station, in a queue, and in the dentist's waiting room. Use the time constructively for writing research.

You can even swap noise notes with other writers. Your writing buddy may be working on a scene set in an abandoned mine-shaft – and you may have notes about the sounds in such a place. Or you may write a scene set in the Brazilian jungle – where she took notes during her trip last year.

Made in the USA
Coppell, TX
05 June 2025